Goats in Trees

The Whys and Why-Nots of
Successful Branding,
Marketing and More

by J. Mark Bangerter

Goats in Trees: The Whys and Why-Nots of Successful Branding, Marketing and More

Copyright © 2011 by J. Mark Bangerter

ISBN: 1467975559

ISBN-13: 978-1467975551

Printed in USA

Cover photography by Staff Sergeant Whitney Houston

For Maverick

Foreword

Branding? What's that? That might be what you're asking yourself if you're considering reading this book on branding. Maybe you're struggling to define your business's brand or maybe you're trying to better communicate your personal brand to clients or potential employers.

You might be wondering what branding is and how on earth you could apply any branding concepts to your business or personal brand, or why you should even try to do this. After all, who cares?

In a nutshell, branding is all the behind-the-scenes thinking that should happen before any marketing or promotion gets underway. I always say that branding isn't rocket science, but it sure isn't easy either. Understanding brand concepts isn't the hard part, but knowing how to apply them into building a strong and memorable brand is a totally different story.

And knowing how to take these concepts and use them to make a brand memorable and relevant to your customer or audience is the key to having a successful brand and something every brand should spend time on. But the fact of the matter is many brands don't spend time on this.

Goats in Trees does a good job of boiling down some of the basic concepts of branding into easy-to-understand and applicable ideas that you can use to develop your brand whether it's for your business or yourself.

So by giving your brand some attention you can stand out from the crowd and really connect with your customers in a more meaningful and relevant way.

Diane Diaz
Full Sail University

Preface

I have been writing Goats in Trees for nigh on two years. It started as a blog. (I do not consider myself a blogger). One day I looked back at my posts and said to myself, "I have got some good stuff here. I should write a book." So yes, you can find some of the pages from this book on my blog. But not the whole book. What I have done here is taken content that I had already written. I organized it. I wrote new content. I organized that. I formatted and edited and now we have Goats in Trees.

This is not *Branding for Dummies*. Goats in Trees is intended to make you think. Even if I told you how to do something and even if I gave you a step-by-step guide, it still comes down to one thing – **you** have to do it. **You** have to be the one to get inspired and get it done.

(Let me qualify my previous statement. There are some things I do write out as a step-by-step process, but they are very basic. **You** still have to do the work. Nothing should take more than three steps to complete. Do not over think.)

I wrote this as a branding book. But you can read it as a cookbook, a book on dancing, a small business book, etc. This book can be anything that you want it to be. If anything, apply this to **Brand You** (a term coined by Tom Peters) and you can use this as a guide to finding a new job. Apply the principles to whatever it is you are doing. Apply them to yourself as a person.

Everyone who reads this is at a different point in his or her life. One might be unemployed and struggling to support his family. One might be a millionaire and looking to expand her empire. There is a different story here for everyone who reads, because each one of us is different. Everyone will take something different away from this.

Goats in Trees is not just about branding. I talk a lot about branding as well as marketing because those are the things that I am passionate about. What are you passionate about? Apply it to that while you are reading.

Goats in Trees is about recognizing the laws that we have to obey (the Whys), what rules are completely bogus, and what we can do to differentiate ourselves from the herd (the Why-Nots).

Like I said, you can apply this to anything that you do. You can pick up this book a year from now and re-read it and you will get something completely different out of it. I write the way that I write to make you think. My telling you what to do is not going to do anything for you. My inspiring you to think will do wonders.

That is my goal with this book. I hope that you can become inspired. I hope that you can find what it is that you are looking for. I hope that you can extract the tiniest tidbit of something that I have said and turn it into the greatest idea this world has ever seen. I would be overjoyed if you were able to take something that I have said and become inspired to greater things.

J. Mark Bangerter
November 14, 2011

CHAPTER 1
Goats in Trees?

Have you ever seen such a thing? There are goats in Morocco that love to eat the leaves from a certain tree.

So what do they do?

They simply climb the tree and eat the leaves. No one ever told them that goats do not climb trees. Mountain goats climb mountains, but I have never heard of a tree goat.

All of my life I knew that goats did not climb trees. No one ever told me that specifically. I just knew it. I knew that goats do not climb trees.

But now, all of a sudden, I have experienced a complete paradigm shift.

I have seen a photograph of a goat in a tree.

I guess it could have been Photoshopped, but I am pretty sure that it wasn't.

Military photographer Staff Sergeant Whitney Houston, who is a friend of mine, took the photo that appears on the cover, while he was stationed in Morocco.

But I always imagined goats as mobile trash compactors. They eat whatever trash they can find on the ground.

They graze and eat grass and weeds.

But "Goats in Trees?"

It just blew my mind.

Are You a Ground Goat or a Tree Goat?

You might say proudly, "I am not a goat!"

Well, this is my book. My name is on the cover. In my book, you are a goat. If you do not like it, you have no business reading any further. (No refunds.) And you are either a Ground Goat or a Tree Goat.

The Ground Goats are the goats that live up to our expectations (which in this case is not a good thing). The Tree Goats do the unexpected.

Are you doing what all the other goats do and graze in the pastures and eat trash?

Or are you climbing the trees that no one else thought possible?

Just because no one has ever done it with his or her brand, does not mean it is impossible. If you can think it, you can do it.

Or else, why would you think of it? You just have to get creative and work a little bit.

As you read this, keep a notebook or voice recorder handy. Make notes in the margins, it is your copy of the book for crying out loud! You paid for it. You will be inspired and you will need to remember that inspiration.

Write it down. Record it. Tap-tap it into your iPad and email it to yourself. Immortalize it somehow…

And then do it

Inspiration has a limited time warranty. If you fail to act on inspiration within a decent amount of time, you do not get to complain when the forces that be give you bad juju. (And they will!) You failed to act. When you are inspired, write it down and then do it ASAP! I'm absolutely serious here.

These are pearls I'm handing to you.

CHAPTER 2
The Goat –
(The Whys)

What is your first thought when you think of Marketing? The 4 P's! Right! Anyone who has ever taken any business course has learned about the 4 P's! And what are they?

Umm........

I got it......

Hold on.....

Product, Price, Place and Promotion, right?

All right! But what does it mean?

> What are the
> Fundamentals of
> Christianity?

- ✓ The Ten Commandments.
- ✓ The Golden Rule.
- ✓ Love your neighbor.
- ✓ Love God.

> What are the
> Fundamentals of Sales?

I'll give you a hint - A, B, C.

Always Be ~~Celling~~ Closing

Can you alter these laws?

You can try, but they are **Fundamental** principles. I am using the word fundamental a lot. What does it mean?

Fundamental comes from the same word root as foundation. Can you build a house without a foundation?

Absolutely!

Will it last?

Absolutely not!

Within each ideology there are certain principles that are universal.

Within the Universe itself, there are laws that are unbreakable.

Within the sphere of branding, these are the things that we cannot change about our brand development process.

(Or whatever else we are working on).

For us here in this book, these are the laws set forth by the Branding Gods in the beginning of time. (Or the Dancing Gods or the Cooking Gods, right?)

Transgress these laws and there are eternal consequences.

Years ago I was working as a real estate broker and I carefully crafted the following statement as part of our company's training manual. My motivation and mindset were in a completely different place at the time, but the principle remains:

Success

Every one of our triumphs results directly from our obedience to specific laws. In order to bring to fruition that which we desire, we must obey the applicable laws. However, we must first learn the laws that govern the results that we desire.

I was mostly referring to being successful in real estate, but it really applies to what I am talking about here.

This is the point that I am trying to get across. We must understand the fundamentals that govern what it is that we are trying to accomplish.

This is essential so that we do not try to Reinvent the Wheel or `Siphon the Bucket`. (*See Chapter 10*)

(It is okay, however, to **Repurpose the Wheel**).

I want to make sure that we all get this.

This is important.

What are the **fundamental** principles for boiling water?

You need the following items:
- ✓ Water
- ✓ Heat
- ✓ Some sort of vessel, usually a pot.

You may know of some super-neat, scientific way to boil water without heat, but for all intents and purposes we are boiling this water in an everyday, average kitchen.

Can you boil water without these three things?

No.

What are the steps?

1. First you put the water in the vessel.
2. Second you put the vessel on the heat.
3. Third, the water boils.

Those are **fundamental** principles. You cannot change them and I cannot change them. What happens if you do not put the water in the vessel and you just put it directly on the heat?

(Well, you will get steam; you just sprinted through the boiling step.)

If we want to lose weight, we must consume fewer calories than we burn.

To save money, we must spend less money than we earn.

CHAPTER 3
The Origin of the Brand

What was the first brand? It might be impossible to say.

Was it when Neanderthal man invented the wheel?

Brand Wheel™?

Or maybe The Club™?

He saw that what he had invented provided him with a considerable benefit and he desired to share that benefit with his tribe. He saw the advantages that his Brand could provide over the other tribes. It would be a lot easier to kill food with a club than a stone, right? I do not know. I do not hunt.

What about Brand Rome™?

Rome was a center of enlightenment. There was a lot of good stuff coming out of Rome. Even Caesar had his own image branded on the gold coins that were used.

During the Renaissance painters, sculptors and builders had to establish their brand or else they would starve.

What will happen to us if we don't establish our brand?

Who was commissioned to paint the Sistine Chapel? Was it a nameless artist who painted portraits of peasants? Who was called upon to create the Statue of David?

Brands have been around for a very long time. Where else do we see brands?

Animals, obviously. Animals were branded so that their origin was known.

What about Brand You™?

You have been Brand You™ since you were born. Every time you meet someone they are forming an opinion of you.

What about that individual at the bar who leaves with someone different every night? What are they branded as? Are they pushing Brand No Standards Here?

Yes and no. They may not be trying to, but others are branding him/her that way.

So what is my point here? Brands have always existed, whether as an individual or as a corporation.

CHAPTER 4
What is Branding?

Marty Neumeier said it best (and I am going to say it again and again):

"Your brand is not what you say it is, your brand is what THEY say it is."

Who Came up With the Fundamentals of Branding?

No one and everyone. We all did. As consumers we all determined what the fundamentals of Branding are.

3 Steps to Defining Your Brand or "Choose, but choose wisely..."

Remember in the movie *Indiana Jones and the Last Crusade* when the knight guarding the Holy Grail says, "You must choose, but choose wisely."

In my experience, one of the most difficult things to do is to choose how to define a new venture. Working with a team can make this even more difficult.

So how do you define what your brand is? First off, *you* do not. Your consumers do. (Turn back a couple of pages to the Marty Neumeier quote.)

But you still have to guide your consumers. You need to be the one to lead them. You need to establish the tribe. The tribe members will start showing up and they will decide what the tribe is. It happens all the time. You might have an amazing idea. You ship it and the consumer can decide that he likes it better for something other than the intended purpose.

So here are the three steps. (You should try to do everything in only three steps).

I do not often give step-by-step guides so pay attention.

Step 1: Brainstorm

I use a mindmap. You can do this on paper or there are a number of free apps out there for mindmapping.

I have used FreeMind –

http://sourceforge.net/projects/freemind

I just downloaded another one, MindNode. It seems to have a bit more aesthetic appeal, but it does not have all the features of FreeMind.

http://www.mindnode.com

Get all of your ideas out. Good and bad. Especially the bad. Get them all down and get them organized however you see fit.

Step 2: Eliminate

Start going through everything that you have put down on paper (or your computer). Find the paths that will lead you to your goals. Eliminate the paths you do not need.

Step 3: Narrow

Narrow your focus. Focus on one aspect or one final outcome. This is your brand. This is what you will take to your consumers. Where do you want to be? You will be most successful if you can focus your energies on one outcome instead of multiple outcomes. Your fans will tell you whether or not you have chosen wisely.

28

CHAPTER 5
Brand Plan

Do you have a brand plan? Having a great idea won't do you any good unless you have a plan. Everyone is always talking about a plan.

- ✓ Your business plan.
- ✓ Your diet plan.
- ✓ Your workout plan.
- ✓ Your planning plan.

There is a reason people will sell you this horse-puckey...

It's good horse-puckey! You need a plan!

This goes hand in hand with **Defining Your Brand**. Use the mindmapping tools I just mentioned to create your plan. Utilize the same steps. Like I said before, you shouldn't need more than three steps to accomplish anything.

- ✓ What is the goal for your Brand? (Notice I said Goal? Singular.)
- ✓ What are you trying to accomplish? (Mission)
- ✓ What steps are you going to take today, tomorrow, next week and so on?
- ✓ What type of message will you send out?
- ✓ What channels will you use to publish and syndicate your message?
- ✓ What platforms will you use?
- ✓ Which formats will you use and how often will you send it out?

These are only a few of the things that you need to include in your plan. Create your plan. Stick to it. Email me your plan and I will review it for you. No strings attached. I'll do it just because I am that awesome.

mark@zapsock.com

CHAPTER 6

Brand Differentiation

Another one of the books I have read recently is *Zag* by Marty Neumeier. First time I read anything from Marty was *The Brand Gap*. I loved it. Marty is one of my heroes.

The Brand Gap is short and to the point and does not aggravate my ADD. *Zag* is the same way. It is brilliant. It is all about brand differentiation.

What are you doing to make your brand different? How do you stand out from the rest of the noise? If your brand is not different, you are wasting your time.

If you want to be successful, you have to differentiate yourself from the rest of the chatter.

Facebook was a huge success. WHY? MySpace was already huge, so why was Facebook able to come along and steal everyone from MySpace? Because it was different.

But they are both social networks, you say. Mark Zuckerburg started Facebook as a network for college students.

And it was **different** than MySpace.

Did you know that there are hundreds and thousands of social networks out there right now? How many can you name? Why haven't you heard of any of them?

Because they are just noise. They are not any different.

There are many strategies to differentiate your brand, but you have to be willing to get creative. You have to be different.

Google+ is a new social network and it has grown faster than any other social network to date. Why is this? I have a two-part theory:

1. It is backed by Google

- ✓ Google is such a strong brand that it is officially a verb.
- ✓ The definition of Google from the Collins English Dictionary is "to search for (something on the Internet) using a search engine."
- ✓ You do not even have to use the Google BRAND search engine to Google something.
- ✓ You can use Yahoo or Bing and Google something on there.

2. It is different. How?

- ✓ You can connect with anyone you want on Google without their permission
- ✓ You can post anything you want and share it with various "Circles"
- ✓ You can "Hangout"
- ✓ It is a "more natural feeling social network."

(However, in many descriptions you will find that people compare various aspects of Google+ to various aspects of Facebook. This lends credibility to the strength of Facebook's brand.)

Do not do what everyone else does.

Find the tree that you like and eat from it... even if no one else is.

CHAPTER 7

Brand Awareness

I'm not that old, but I am from an old school generation. I still remember the times when we didn't have the Internet in the home. We didn't even have a computer.

The most high tech devices in our home were:

- ✓ Our top loading VCR
- ✓ The 8-bit NES
- ✓ My dad's work pager

And my mom had a word processor. In fact, she was able to sell her services as a typist. Now everyone's a typist.

Death of the Antenna Ball

Do you remember these? They still have some at various places. Were they antenna balls or antenna toppers? Whatever you want to call them. I guess a ball would be a topper but a topper wouldn't necessarily be a ball.

What does this have to do with anything? Antenna balls were awesome! I remember when you would see half the cars on the road with a 76 Station antenna ball. The sign for the gas station itself was a ginormous antenna ball! I do not remember if you had to buy them or if they gave them away free, but it was one of the most ingenious forms of increasing brand awareness.

Then everyone jumped on the bandwagon. Then came the death of the antenna ball. Not all cars have aerial antennas anymore. Radio is not all analog anymore.

So what will the next "antenna ball" be? Will it be your idea? What are you doing to create Brand Awareness?

CHAPTER 8
Your Brand Niche

Hyper Niche Flat Tops?

Those were the first words that came to me when I saw the barbershop on the following page.

Now I realize that those first words were terrible. I can recognize a bad idea. It should have been "Micro-Niche Flat-Tops."

Senior rates. Flat tops.

Senior rates are good for the location. My city has a high population of senior citizens, so that makes sense. Seniors come in every other week to get their hair cut and they only have a half a head of hair.

Makes sense.

But flat tops? I haven't seen someone with a flat top in a while. You know how they do a flat top? A giant flat comb and clippers. Vóilá! So is this guy a genius or stuck in the 90s?

I say he's a genius.

Where else would you go to get a flat top? Have you established your brand this way? What do you do to target a micro niche? Are you doing something different than everyone else, or are you just adding to the noise?

This is for you to decide. I cannot tell what your niche is. Your niche has to be something that you are passionate about.

Let Me Tell You About My Wife

I love my wife. She is very creative. She is determined and stubborn. She gets it done. She is an inspiration to me. We have three children. Two girls and a baby boy. When the older girl was born, my wife was having a hard time finding hair accessories that she liked and that were affordable. So what did she do? She figured out how to make hair accessories.

She was making hair bows and headbands for our girls and people would ask her, "Where can I get something like that?"

She started making them for her friends for their baby showers and their children's birthdays.

More people started asking about them. So she started a website. She started taking custom orders. She makes high-quality hand-made hair accessories for girls. She soon had a decent business going for herself. People started asking her if she would teach them how to make the bows. So she did. She started doing classes. She makes more money teaching classes than she ever did selling bows.

One of the women, who she had taught how to make bows, started her own business and started stealing business from my wife! This upset my wife as you can imagine.

I sat down with her and analyzed her business model, as I tend to do with everyone whether they like it or not.

I said, "Why compete with her? Her bows aren't that great. You know that. Everyone else is going to see that. You have something better going on. You are not a bow maker. You are *the* Bow Guru(ess). You are the master. People must come to you to learn how to make bows. Capitalize on that. Make that your niche."

And she did.

She focused on teaching others how to make bows. That was her primary service that she offered.

And what happened?

Her bow sales increased! They nearly doubled. She almost couldn't keep up with the work.

I say to her sometimes, "Why are you still making the bows? Why don't you outsource it to China or India? Your profit-margin would be that much higher, you could sell more bows and you would not have to spend so much time making the bows."

She said, "No. I enjoy making the bows. I don't want the quality of my bows to suffer because they are being mass-produced. I am doing something that I love."

She is doing something that she is passionate about. She found her niche.

By the way, do you say "neeshe" or "nitch"? I say "nitch." I cannot stand the other way.

CHAPTER 9

Why I Hate Marketing

Okay, so I do not really hate marketing. But, there is one aspect of marketing that is so essential, but it is also one of the most tedious. I have grouped this area under Research & Testing. I know that these are two separate things, but they are the two areas that I dread the most.

Let's first take a look at research.

Research

Having never done it, would you ever try to bake a cake without looking for a recipe or seeking instruction? Would you go white water rafting or climb Mt. Everest without, at the very least, consulting a guidebook? You would most likely even hire a guide.

Do you ever make a purchase without trying to find out something about the product and then search for a similar product or a better price for the same product? Probably, but then you have also most likely experienced the remorse that accompanies the revelation of, "Oh, I got the same thing at XYZ Store for $100 more!" This is why research is so essential to any branding or marketing venture.

You need to know who wants to buy your product or service.

- ✓ Where are they?
- ✓ How do you reach them?
- ✓ How much are they willing to pay?
- ✓ Where can you find similar products?

You must know your competition.

Entire volumes have been written about marketing research alone. Learn to do it and you will love it. If you say, "Forget it," you may regret it.

You also need to know how people are responding to your brand. You may find out that they think that your brand is something completely different than what you intended it to be. And that's okay.

Testing

Once again many, many books have been written about testing. Testing is what you do once you have launched your campaign. Why testing? Because you must know if your campaign is working!

- ✓ Where are you getting the most hits?
- ✓ Where do your customers come from?
- ✓ What pages are creating the most conversions?

Testing is research **after** you have launched your campaign. If you do not do testing, you are wasting your marketing dollars.

I recommend that anyone who is looking to start their own business learn about these two aspects of marketing. These are the things that separate the winners from the bankrupt.

Real World Application

I cannot tell you what to do now. You know what to do. It is in you to do it. But keep reading; we are not done yet.

CHAPTER 10
The Ground Goat
(The Rules)

There is a big difference between *the Fundamentals* and *the Rules*. We must understand this in order to be successful. Fundamentals do not change. They are universal laws. That is why it is essential to respect their authority.

Rules have been put in place by those who wish to justify their narrow thinking. I am not condoning the breaking of rules.

You still need to look both ways before crossing the street and wash your hands after using the restroom. I am establishing that there are *Rules*.

The *Rules* are those walls that we have erected to be the boundaries to our creativity and thinking. We allow these rules to justify our inaction.

- ✓ The *Rules* once stated that the Earth was the center of the known universe.
- ✓ The *Rules* once stated that the world was flat.
- ✓ The *Rules* once stated that leaving meat out overnight caused little faeries to turn it into bugs.
- ✓ The *Rules* once stated that the Internet was a bad idea.
- ✓ The *Rules* once stated that blacks and whites could not function together in society.

The *Rules* are limitations that hinder our creative inner beast. Many do not understand the Fundamentals and so they create rules in order for them to feel like they are accomplishing something; when in fact, all they are doing is limiting their own thinking and your thinking as well.

The fundamentals must be applied correctly. Or else we are just Siphoning the Bucket.

Siphoning the Bucket

During my time as a missionary in Uruguay over eight years ago, I found myself in a very interesting situation. We were preparing for a baptismal service. The baptistery was a small pool inside the church building, but the water didn't drain into a sewer line.

It had to be pumped out so as not to fill the septic tank up too rapidly. However, this time the pump wasn't working and there was water still in it from the previous two weeks.

Disgusting, right?

We had to figure out a way to get the water out.

I had the idea to try a siphon.

If you do not know what a siphon is or how it works, it is a way to move water (liquid) through a length of hose or pipe utilizing the forces of gravity and suction.

The trick to getting it right is that the end of the hose where the water comes out has to be lower than the end where the water goes into the hose.

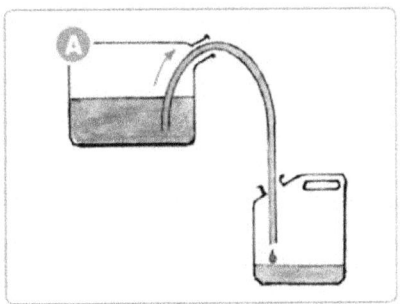

So back to the story we found a length of hose and stuck it down in the pool. We took the other end out to the street, which was pretty low, but not quite low enough.

After trying to make this work for an hour or so, we gave up on the idea and got some buckets to get the water out. This way we could bucket the water out and either pour it down the toilet or into the drain in the floor.

One of the church members who was there helping us, had the brilliant idea to "siphon the bucket." He really wanted to find a way to make that siphon work. In fact he was obsessing on this one idea so much, that it blinded him to everything else. His idea was to dip the bucket into the pool to fill it up, set the bucket on the side of the pool and siphon the water out of the bucket. (A standard 5-gallon bucket)

This would make the end of the hose lower than the other end of the hose, causing the siphon to work.

I just looked at him.

Do you see the problem? I hope so

Are you **siphoning the bucket**?

Are you so dependent upon a piece of technology or a method or a set way of thinking that even when the situation calls for some improvisation you still want to stick to what you know?

Think outside the box. Create paradigm shifts. Be a thought leader. Do not siphon the bucket.

> The Pizzeria Theorem:
> Absolute Failure For You
> and Your Brand in 30 Days
> or Less!

So I have been noticing a lot of businesses going under lately. Have you seen this trend? Is it due to the economy?

Personally I do not think so.

At least not completely.

A Story

I still live in the same town where I grew up. There was a local pizza place called Premier Pizza. I do not think I actually ever ate there, but I heard it was pretty popular.

I drove by there recently and noticed that Premier Pizza is no longer there. It's something else. It's another pizza place. Now it's entirely possible that the owner changed the name, but very unlikely.

The Reason

So assuming Premier Pizza has quietly gone the way of the buffalo, why? Perhaps it was the location? Perhaps it is the fact that there are several pizza places around town that offer $5 pizzas. I didn't see any signs indicating that they were competing with the $5 pizza biz.

To me it just does not seem like a very good idea to invest in the exact same business that had failed there before.

This tells me that it wasn't the economy so much as it was a failure to evolve.

What are you doing
to adapt?

(Adapt ≠ Conform)

Or are you going to just keep doing
what the other lemmings do?

CHAPTER 11
The Marketing Industry is Finished

Well, maybe not.

But are we really marketing?

What is marketing? It is not sales. Sales is sales and marketing is marketing. I hated it when I was looking for a marketing gig and everyone would post sales jobs in the marketing section.

But I do not want to define something by what it is not.

Marketing is communication.

Do not be salesmen.

Do not be billboards.

Be marketers.

Communicate and engage.

As Brian Solis says, "Engage or Die"

Pushing works, but they will resent you. Who has the worst rep amongst salesmen? Used car salesmen? Real estate agents? You hate them, but you go to them. But do you ever go back to the same one again?

Pushy marketers are worse than pushy salesmen.

Pull

What do people really want? They want to know that you care. Take the extra minute to ask someone how he or she is. Take the extra five minutes to get to know someone. It will make all the difference.

You will pull them to you and they will keep coming back to you. Once again, social media is not marketing. It is a tool we use to communicate.

Please do not confuse what I am saying with the actual concept of Push vs. Pull Marketing. I am talking about pushing people away and pulling them in to you via communication and relationship building.

This leads me to my next point.

CHAPTER 12

I Despise Social Media

I have been thinking about this for a long time. I do not actually despise social media, but I do have a love/hate relationship with it.

Let me explain.

I did my undergraduate work in Marketing. My graduate studies are in Internet Marketing.

I have studied the best of both worlds and have come to appreciate that happy place where the two collide in harmony.

Social media has absolutely revolutionized the way that marketing and brand development take place. But once again, it is a tool.

Advertising dollars are often more wisely invested in Facebook ads than in a newspaper. Social Media allows businesses to reach out to micro-niche markets.

It's beautiful.

So why the hate? I think that some people may be putting too much focus on Social Media strategy.

Also, everyone and anyone with a Twitter account is all of a sudden a Social Media Guru.

Just because someone knows how to tweet, does not make him or her an expert.

So watch out for these guys.

Another Story

I was recently speaking with a prospective client. He has been in business for a very long time. He has been successful. He wanted to learn how to market with Facebook.

My first thought was, "Sure."

My second thought was, "You cannot market with Facebook. Facebook is a means of engaging your consumers."

And as I thought about it more, I realized that is what marketing is [supposed to be].

However, too many people think that having a Facebook Page and a Twitter account is Marketing.

[Facebook ≠ Marketing]

Facebook can be a tool that you use for marketing. This is my plea for marketers to get back to being marketers.

Social Media is not a cure-all/cover-all strategy for marketing. There are so many more aspects of Marketing *and* Internet Marketing that cannot be taken care of with a Facebook page and a blog. I guess somewhere along the line someone smart talked about using Facebook within his brand messaging strategy and someone read it and thought that was all he needed to do.

Moderation my friends.

You will learn.

CHAPTER 13
Epic Branding Fail

Al and Laura Ries authored one of the greatest texts on branding that I have read. It is called, "The 22 Immutable Laws of Branding." The 22 Laws are great guidelines for anyone who is thinking of starting a business, has recently started a business, or is currently involved in a business- yes, everyone.

Here I just want to talk about the
first two laws.

You can find all 22 laws in the book or at the Ries'
website:

*http://synergynet.com/artman/publish/marketing_reso
urces/branding_laws.shtml*

The following is taken from the website:

> "1. The Law of Expansion: The
> power of a brand is inversely
> proportional to its scope.
> Trying to be all things to all
> people undermines the power of
> the brand.

"The strength of brands lies in becoming synonymous with a single category. Brands that spread themselves across categories lose brand focus, identity, and ultimately market share.

"2. The Law of Contraction: A brand becomes stronger when you narrow its focus. By narrowing the focus to a single category, a brand can achieve extraordinary success. Starbucks, Subway and Dominos Pizza became category killers when they narrowed their focus."

So what do you suppose I thought a while back when I saw that El Pollo Loco started serving Sirloin Steak?

That's right.

El Pollo Loco, who originally only served grilled chicken, is [*was*] now serving steak. In case you do not know, "Pollo" is "chicken" in Spanish.

El Pollo Loco means "The Crazy Chicken."

So why would a chicken restaurant serve steak?

They have adapted a *Rule*.

Instead of making the chicken better or making more people aware of the chicken, they are attracting the steak lovers. Leave the steak lovers alone.

Go home. Go cook your chicken.

As my father said after I told him about this:

"That must be one crazy chicken if you can get sirloin steak from it!"

BREAK

Knowing When to Quit

J.,

We noticed you haven't logged in for **523 days**. We have added many features since your last visit, and we hope you login today to take a look.

Here are some examples of what thousands of other professionals are doing with us:

- Connecting with potential customers using our "Direct Match" feature.
- Promoting their services and products through our Press Distribution service.
- Using our Direct Mail Service to target members by industry, region or custom search.
- Leverage our E-Mail Marketing service to send professional emails to your contacts.

Get started: Login Now.

Really? 523 Days? I do not know if I am coming back. But thanks for trying. This was a real email that I received. What does it have to do with anything? Nothing. It just exudes pure epic fail.

CHAPTER 14
The Tree Goat
(The Why-Nots)

In order to be successful we need to abide by the *Fundamentals* but play outside the rules. Tim Ferriss became a successful kickboxing champ by exploiting loopholes in the basic fundamentals of kickboxing that said that you could win by throwing or pushing your opponent outside the ring.

However, there was a *Rule* in place that this shouldn't be done. But he didn't play by the *Rules*. He threw his opponents outside the ring and won.

When you have an idea, ask yourself, "Is this a good idea?" And then answer yourself, "Why not?"

```
i.e
```

John has an idea to invent a new product. He is scared of failing. (We have ALL been there.) He tells a friend his idea, and his friend says that it stinks. But John knows that it could potentially be great. He just needs to have a little faith in himself and in the inspiration that he has received. So he says, "Why not? What is keeping me from doing this? Why not do this? I am going to do it!"

Think of the "Why-Nots" as a positive thing.

And also learn to recognize when someone is telling you that your idea stinks because in actuality it stinks and when someone is telling you that your idea stinks because they know that they will never have the guts to pull it off.

The Wheel is there. It is the *Fundamental*. You can repurpose it, but you cannot change it. Keep reading for some ideas on how you can get in the tree.

Read This and Then Tell Me How You Feel

From my blog:

Freebies! Get your freebies here! | ZAPSOCK

I have been reading Chris Anderson's "Free."

I am loving it.

It is very informational and exceptionally insightful.

As I was reading it I had an idea, and I am going to give it to you for FREE.

Here it is, I hope someone takes this idea and runs with it.

Get some investors to invest some of their hard earned $$$.

Build (or purchase) a movie theatre.

You won't need to focus on fancy stadium seating or anything like that.

You GIVE the popcorn away to everyone. That's right everyone.

Every ticket stub comes with a coupon for a free medium popcorn.

Not small, medium.

I do not really feel like elaborating on why this is such an ingenius idea, but I will.

- Everyone goes through your concession line.
- People will be more prone to purchase other items: candy, soda, and hot dogs.
- The lines for the concessions will be longer, so you have ads playing on monitors located in the lines.
- Not just up on the walls.
- More people will come to your theatre because you have free popcorn.

Why does this make sense?

Because everyone knows that a 20 ounce serving of popcorn is NOT worth $5.00.

It is not even worth 5 cents.

Your investment into this is minimal, but the returns will be extraordinary.

I truly hope someone does this.

By the way, I hate popcorn.

And discuss amongst yourselves...

How did that make you feel? Was it uncomfortable? I hope so.

It should have been a thorn in your backside.

Why would you give something away that is so profitable?

Because the returns will be greater.

It hasn't been done before. I guarantee you that people will eat this up. Now was I talking about a literal movie theater in this post?

You bet!

But how can you apply this to what you are doing? You may not have to give anything away for free, but what can you do to step outside yourself and do something other than what is expected of you?

Just a Thought | ZAPSOCK

It is a tough job market out there.

Unemployment rates are sky high.

One of the biggest determining factors when employers are reviewing applicants is not necessarily a degree, it's experience.

A degree is important, but if you have no experience, do you know what that means to a potential employer?

$$$ MONEY $$$

They have to spend lots of it in order to train you to do the job right.

If they can hire someone who already knows what they are doing, that person is going to become profitable much sooner.

Also, what if the inexperienced candidate does not work out?

All the wages they paid you during your training, WASTED.

That is not something that anyone wants to do right now.

With hundreds of applicants, employers are extremely picky with who they are hiring.

Catch 22 right?

So how do you get experience?

Start your own business.

Do you want a job teaching?

Start tutoring kids.

Do it for free.

Experience is worth so much more.

Do you want a job as a business executive?

Start a consultation business.

Offer your services to these businesses for free.

You will gain invaluable experience, exceptional knowledge and you may even like running your own business.

If there are not any opportunities, make some.

(And you can put it all on your resume!)

Hourly Wage Jobs

As a society we teach our youth to get a minimum wage job and start from the bottom and work their way up. I have no problem with this. But this is getting even harder now with the "Notification Generation." Youth today rarely decide to be pro-active. It seems that they cannot act without first getting a text, Facebook notification, tweet or whatever.

We teach them to work hard. Again, no problem. We teach them that as long as they are on the clock, they will get paid.

I have a problem with this.

We make them take a half hour lunch break and two fifteen minute breaks. Even if they do not want to.

I have a problem with this!

We teach them that as long as they show up, they will get paid.

I have a problem with this!

Please explain to me how this makes sense. I show up to work and do nothing. My boss pays me because, "Hey, I'm punctual!"

Awesome-sauce.

We are not incentivizing our employees. Or perhaps we are just not offering the right incentives. We teach them to do things a certain way and if they do it any other way it is bad. Even if it saves us more money and is more efficient.

My buddy bought a fast-food sandwich shop. He needs to hire employees.

I said, "Buddy, why not hire your employees on commission? They can get paid per sandwich."

Says my buddy to me, "I can't. I have to pay them minimum wage. It's the law."

I said, "Buddy, not if they are 1099 independent contractors?"

Do you think that would fly? Independent sandwich sales? Why not? I won't naysay it.

CHAPTER 15
Killing Your High Score

Have you ever played Pac-Man? Donkey Kong? Super Mario Bros? I'm sure you have some sort of game on your smart phone where the objective is to achieve the highest possible score. In some of these games it is the only objective.

Have you played the helicopter game? All you do is fly for as long as you possibly can. The game is programmed to continue indefinitely as long as you do not crash. It was my favorite game on my old Palm Pré. (What's Palm?)

When we play these games, we tend to beat our high score a little bit more each time. Just a little bit.

Is it because we are getting better?

Sure!

Is it because we are learning from our past mistakes?

Absolutely!

But I think there's more.

I have found that it is human nature to subconsciously give up once we have reached a predetermined threshold, or "high score." We find it is okay to achieve this same score. Even coming up short, as long as it is within an unspoken proximity, is acceptable. Beating the high score by the smallest margin is, in our primitive ape brain, a fantastic achievement worthy of the highest honors.

When you are developing a new brand, are you trying to eke your way past the "high score?" Are you satisfied with creating something that falls short, but within the acceptable range? Or do you seek to kill the high score? Slaughter the status quo?

Google didn't create a search engine that was on par with existing algorithms - they established an empire.

When you search for something on the interwebs, you do not "Yahoo! it", you do not "Ask Jeeves" and you definitely do not "Bing it." No matter which search engine we are using, we "Google it."

You want to be the next Sergei? Or the next Zuckmeister?

Do **not** do what they have already done.

Do not crash the helicopter in the exact same spot each time.

Destroy the high score.

Drop a nuke on it.

CHAPTER 16
Being a Brand Leader

Have you read the Brand Gap by Marty Neumeier yet? (Of course not, you are still reading this. Go pick it up as soon as you are done with this.) In it Mr. Neumeier says that your brand is not what YOU say it is, it's what THEY say it is. (Did you notice that I keep repeating this? Must be important.)

They, in this statement, are your consumers.

It's the same with leadership. Just because *you* say you are a leader or your business card says you are, does not make you a leader. Just because you have thousands of followers on Twitter or on your super-spiffy NING network, that does not make you a leader. You may be the CEO of a corporation with over 10,000 employees and you might not be a leader. You are only a leader if your followers say you are. Just the fact that there are followers is not enough to make you a leader.

If your followers love you and respect you, only then are you a leader. A leader attracts others with kindness and self-sacrifice. This attraction is magnetic. It is atomic. A true leader will always put his followers' interests before his own.

There is an actual, physical attraction (not necessarily romantic or sexual) between the leader and follower.

How attractive are you as a leader?

CHAPTER 17

The Often Overlooked Art of Branding

Where Are You At?

It is my experience that most companies, products or services are at one of three places when it comes to the Art of Branding:

1. It is completely overlooked,
2. It is done completely wrong, due to misunderstanding what branding actually is, or
3. It is utilized correctly and they are successful at building their brand.

Those who fall under #3, they are the ones at the top.

So What is Branding Again?

Yes. We are going over this again. This is a review segment before we go into the next few chapters. What would you say branding is off the top of your head? Take a wild guess if you do not know or do not remember. What was the first word that came to your head?

✓ Logo?
✓ Icon?
✓ Branding Iron?
✓ Symbol?

No, no, no and no.

It is not a word nor is it a symbol.

A brand is defined as the gut feeling that the consumer has about your company, product or service, right? So how do you define your brand now?

Trick question.

CHAPTER 18

The Often Overlooked Art of Storytelling

I enjoy being creative and coming up with ways to be different. What about storytelling? It is such an important part of branding. Many times we do not really think of storytelling when we think of branding. But let's take a look at a few campaigns that have effectively used storytelling:

The Most Interesting Man in the World

http://www.dosequis.com

I do not drink alcohol, but Dos Equis has one of the greatest campaigns overall as well as superior use of the art of storytelling. They have created a man known only as "The Most Interesting Man in the World." And he is indeed.

The Most Interesting Man in the World is nameless. He has a face. It is the face of a tough, older Latino man. He states at the end of the ads, "I do not always drink beer, but when I do, I prefer Dos Equis."

The Most Interesting Man in the World (TMIMITW) is endorsing Dos Equis! This has even spawned an Internet meme where people take an image of TMIMITW and add their own caption such as, "I do not always go to the gym, but when I do, I post it on Facebook."

Everyone knows this campaign. Even if they do not drink the beer, they know the campaign.

Scarlet

http://www.youtube.com/lgScarletTVseries

When you get a chance watch this commercial. The link goes to the YouTube channel where there are five different videos that you can watch. This is another one that absolutely nailed the use of storytelling, however, it didn't last. But that is okay. It was only used up until the product launch.

LG was launching their new Scarlet TVs and they promoted "Scarlet" like a new TV series. Ingenius. Scarlet appeared to be the main character in a new sexy, spy TV show. There are scenes of the actress walking down the red carpet. There is a producer shouting, "I want to put her in every home."

Why was this campaign so great? They took a physical product, and they gave it a human face. They created buzz using a story. In my opinion, a brilliant campaign for a launch. They only gave a little bit of info, but not too much. Get everyone interested and then hit him with the truth!

http://www.allstate.com/mayhem-is-everywhere.aspx

Allstate came out with a great campaign maybe about a year ago with an actor who is "Mayhem." These ads are hilarious. Mayhem causes all kinds of, well, mayhem. He is a raccoon having babies in your attic. He is a lightening storm that causes a tree to fall on your car. He is your blind spot while driving on the freeway (one of my personal favorites and one that I have attempted to reenact).

Once again, we see someone putting a face to something that normally does not have one. This is the beauty of storytelling.

So why is storytelling so important? It helps customers relate on an emotional level. Whether that emotion is humor, excitement, sadness, suspense or whatever it may be. Help them feel emotions. The human animal is an emotional beast. And remember, it does not HAVE to be a fictitious story. Maybe a true story is what your customers will relate with best.

Why do you think businesses use testimonials from clients?

That is storytelling!

CHAPTER 19

Do not Market Like a Marketer

Well how do you (or do you not) do that?

What do many marketers, designers, developers and even business owners do? They do what *they* want. They do not do what the end user or consumer wants.

When you are designing a product, service or a website, ask yourself, "Is this what I want or is this what my client wants?" If you are doing it for yourself, you are doing it for the wrong reasons.

Do not add a feature just because it is flashy or cool. Whatever you are doing, do it well, but make sure that you know what your clients want. Sound like too much work?

You're in the wrong

CHAPTER 20
Good Idea/Bad Idea

When I was a kid there was a cartoon show called Animaniacs. I think that this is a show that will only be remembered by those who are close to my own age. It wasn't on very long, but it was the show that first featured "Pinky and the Brain."

There was a segment that they would do called "Good Idea/Bad Idea." It was some quirky little bit about how walking your dog was a good idea but having your dog walk you was a bad idea. So pretty ridiculous, right?

Take a look at your ideas for your brand. Lay them out there on index cards. Put them into two piles labeled, Good Idea and Bad Idea. But make sure you are putting them in the right pile. Ask yourself why are you putting each idea where you are putting it. Some ideas may look pretty bad at first. But it has been my experience that the ideas that seem pretty bad at first, many times work out the best.

Ask others. We need the criticism from others in order to grow. Take them your good ideas and see what they say.

As Stephen Pressfield says in his book *The War of Art*, a true friend will tell you when you have a bad idea. He will tell you when something sucks. You do not need yes men to blow smoke.

CHAPTER 21

Share Engine Optimization (SHEO)

What is this? SHEO? Do not say "Shee-yo" say "Esh-E-O." Get it? Like S-E-O, but it's SH-E-O.

Share Engine Optimization.

But what is a share engine?

You know what it is.

It is:

- ✓ Facebook
- ✓ Google+
- ✓ Twitter
- ✓ Digg
- ✓ Delicious
- ✓ LinkedIn
- ✓ StumbleUpon
- ✓ Reddit
- ✓ MySpace
- ✓ Blogger
- ✓ Wordpress
- ✓ Tumblr
- ✓ Flickr
- ✓ YouTube
- ✓ Vimeo
- ✓ Viddler
- ✓ It is also the good old fashioned water cooler.

But why?

Facebook recently surpassed Google as the most visited site on the Internet. SEO is still important, do not get me wrong. But you also need to focus on your SHEO. Increase your shareability. Some things to remember:

Be Concise

Internet users skim. They do not read. Create naturally flowing content that is to the point. Use bullet points and headers.

Make it Different

Make sure you are not recycling yesterday's garbage. People want the latest and the greatest. Set up some Google News and Blog feeds on your topics so that you can share the latest news first(ish).

Photo & Video

Remember, if you are going to share photo and video, do not upload 400 photos to one blog post with a paragraph in between each photo, unless you are writing a mom blog. Videos, keep them short, but engage people within the first few seconds or else they will move on.

Gamification

I just read an article yesterday about gamification. Gamification is the process by which you turn your business, site, and marketing efforts into a game. You know Foursquare right? You get badges for checking in at physical locations. Virtual rewards and recognition for interacting with a business. Gamification increases engagement with customers as well as employees.

The article I read yesterday said that by 2014, 70% of the worlds top businesses will be utilizing some sort of app or widget to engage consumers. By mid 2012, 20% of the top companies will be doing this. I think it is time to bring on the gamification.

How does this apply to SHEO? You can reward your users with virtual currency for sharing your content. You are incentivizing them.

Gamification is the next big thing. You heard it here. (And probably somewhere else too.)

CHAPTER 22

Stopping World Hunger With Your Brand

I see a lot of Pages and Groups on Facebook that are called, "I bet I can find 1,000,000 people who want to stop world hunger" or "I bet I can find 1,000,000 people who want to end homelessness."

I do not join these groups.

Why?

Because I do not see what these Facebook groups are doing to actually combat these problems besides talking about it.

I join a group and/or like a page it shows everyone that I want to stop world hunger, but what am I actually doing to get it done? People who think that they are actually doing something are deluded virtual-philanthropists.

Their false charity is currency that cannot be cashed in to truly help someone in need. I think that these types of groups should charge $1 for every person that joins the group. Can you imagine the power of that?

One million dollars raised in a matter of weeks for whatever cause? And all you have to do is have people drop $1 into PayPal. The only problem that I see with it is scam artists.

How do we sort out the cons from the causes?

What do you think? There has to be some way to do this. I'll let you think on it.

If you can end world hunger with Facebook, imagine what you can do with your own brand.

Take these ideas.

I have published them for you.

Be different.

Be creative.

Act now!

Everyday we make the choice to do or not to do those things which will attract Success. Success then makes the choice of whether or not it will find us. If we choose not to do those things which attract Success, we leave Success no choice but to find someone else who is more attractive.

Looking Forward... A Sneak
Peek at What's to Come...

CHAPTER 1

Brand Development 2.0

I had lunch with my good friend Tyler Jorgenson a little while back and he inspired me to make some changes. Instead of being a small business marketing consultant, I am now a Brand Development 2.0 consultant. Why? Because I love branding. I am passionate about it.

That is what Tyler inspired me to do. He told me that you have to do what you are passionate about. Brand Development 2.0 is all about creating your brand in this new era of social media, tablets and instant gratification. It is about listening to your customers.

It is allowing them to define your brand.

Not you.

You were given two ears and one mouth. You should be listening to your customers twice as much as you are speaking to them.

Why did I do this?

I am trying to apply my own teachings to my own consultation practice. How can I ask anyone to do anything that I am not willing to do myself?

.....

Giving Credit Where Credit is Due

I was inspired by many people to write this book. The authors that I have referenced and/or that have inspired me to complete this book are:

Stephen Pressfield

Al & Laura Ries

Marty Neumeier

Seth Godin

Brian Solis

Chris Anderson

Timothy Ferriss

Support them. Buy their books.

About the Author

J. Mark Bangerter was raised in sunny Southern California where he still lives with his wife and three children. Mark is the original Branding Rebel and the founder of Zapsock, a brand development consultancy that focuses on creating paradigm shifts and exploring new paths. You can find out more at:

www.zapsock.com

mark@zapsock.com